Be Well

to Lead Well

A Self-Coaching Guide
to Support Personal
Development and Well-being
at Work

Dr. Waajida L. Small

Printed in the United States of America.

For more information, or to book an event, contact :

info@waajidasmall.com

www.waajidasmall.com

Book and Cover Design by Marla Durden

Copy Editing by Elita Thomas

ISBN – 979-8-9901574-0-8

First Edition: May 2024

Table of Contents

Introduction

There is a debate out in the work world about what it means to be your "whole self" and a question regarding whether someone can truly bring their whole self to work. One school of thought believes that your whole self is your authentic self. It means bringing every part of your personality, hopes, dreams, aspirations, and fears even if they don't align with, or are relevant to what you do. The second one thinks it is better to be fully present in the workplace; being focused on achieving the goals you've set for yourself and not letting any outside influences distract, detract, or deter you from doing so. A third, not so disputed, thought is that being your whole self is a combination of the two.

In his Ted Talk, "Bring Your Whole Self to Work," Mike Robbins talks about the importance of courage and the role it plays on how we should show up and bring all of who we are to the work that we do. He also talks about why we need to embrace vulnerability and to let go of our "attachment to what other people think about us". On the flip side, to build work environments where we feel safe enough to bring our whole selves, we as individuals have to commit to collaboration with the teams and organizations in which we work.

This can be created by creating a safe space and being compassionate and 1) a high level of healthy expectations (expecting excellence) and 2) a high level of nurturance (caring about people). But like an organization's commitment to our well-being, we must also make a commitment to ourselves to work on ourselves and to challenge ourselves to create lives, personal and otherwise, where we can thrive. It can be overwhelming to consider the often bifurcated way of thinking when it comes to the work and life balance. We need to try to identify the how, the why, the when, and the what to really allow ourselves to have full thriving lives at home and at work.

Then, what happens when we become overwhelmed? Well, nothing. Overwhelm often forces us to shut down and stop moving forward. But, if we are confident in who we are, appreciate the value we bring to all of the spaces we enter, and have the tools and resources to help us navigate challenges as they arise, nothing can prevent us from creating healthy whole lives for ourselves.

What does it mean to be well at work?

Let's start off with the basic definition of well-being. It is the holistic state of mental, emotional, and physical health. According to Gallup's global research there are five elements of well-being that add up to a thriving life:

- Career well-being: You like what you do every day.
- Social well-being: You have meaningful friendships in your life.
- Financial well-being: You manage your money well.
- Physical well-being: You have energy to get things done.
- Community well-being: You like where you live.

Collectively, well-being can be defined as the combination of factors that affect quality of work, morale, interpersonal relationships, goal achievement, and outcomes.

In this book, being well in the workplace refers to well-being as it relates to the aspects of your work life. This is usually described as occupational wellness, which often refers to the ability to obtain balance between your work and personal life and results in a sense of personal satisfaction, good health, and financial reward. How well one is at work often influences how they develop in their occupation. This includes opportunities for professional development, career advancement, alignment of purpose, and increases in compensation.

Occupational well-being is important because it is an aspect of mental wellness which everyone in the workplace needs to be equipped with to deal with work-related stressors and productivity issues to reach their full potential. This book provides readers with a guide to do the internal work required to develop their overall well-being so that they can thrive in the workplace.

What is self-coaching and what are its benefits?

The general philosophy in the coaching world is that we can solve our own problems. When you think about coaching, in general, the primary goal of the coach is to ask the client questions to elicit insight into their thoughts and feelings about their life, work, leadership, and whatever the person is being coached on. Self-coaching is the same thing, except you are guiding yourself and asking yourself questions that elicit insight. With self-coaching, you are guiding your own growth and development in either or both of your personal and professional lives. It is guiding your thinking in a way that is structured, and it helps change your perspective away from problem solving and toward solution finding.

Self-coaching is beneficial for several reasons. Chief among them is the development of the skill of asking yourself questions to improve your self-awareness which gives rise to positive actions. It helps to open your thinking to the possible actions you can take that will help you make progress toward achieving your goals.

Through self-coaching you learn to listen to yourself and be confident that you are capable of finding the solutions you need to overcome the obstacles you face, and to open up opportunities for your growth and development.

What you can expect from this book

As a self-coaching guide, each chapter provides strategies, guidance, and "coach yourself questions" (CYQs) prompts to help you begin developing goals around specific areas to support your overall well-being at work. Recommendations for goals are provided at the end of each chapter.

There is an associated action plan for each goal. The action plan includes the following:

- **The goal** - This is the goal you have identified.

- **Start and end date** - When you expect to begin working on the goal and when you expect to be finished.

- **A motivating affirmation** - This can be a quote, saying, mantra, affirmation, or anything that will keep you motivated to continue working on the goal.

- **Action steps and the start and completion dates for each action** - The specific actions you need to take to achieve the goal, and the start and end dates for each.

- **Any obstacles you foresee that may impede your ability to achieve the goal** - Anything that may get in your way of completing the goal.

- **Possible solutions to the obstacle** - Ways in which you can overcome the identified obstacle.

- **The eventual outcome of the goal** - What you have been able to achieve in relation to the identified goal.

Throughout this book there are also other activities, worksheets, and prompts that will help you to dig deeper into your thoughts and actions about specific topics to supplement your goals. Use these resources as you see fit. Start from the beginning or skip around. This book is designed to support you wherever you are in your development journey.

A Starting Point

As a starting point to kick off your wellness journey, complete the "Wheel of Work." The wheel of work is a visual representation of the important areas of your work life at once. This is a bird's eye view that will help you better understand which areas of your work life are flourishing and which ones may need more work. It is a tool that helps you better understand what you can do to improve your work experience.

When we are satisfied in all of our areas of our work, we will find that our sense of well-being and wholeness are magnified. This is because dissatisfaction with one or more areas of our work experience, environment, or our opportunities for development often causes the type of stress and burnout that prevents us from being well or engaging in activities that develop our whole selves.

Before you dive into the book, take a moment to think about the 8 work categories in the wheel below. Rate them from 1 - 10. One is a category in which you are totally unsatisfied, and a 10 is a category in which you are completely satisfied. As you read and work through the book and complete the corresponding activities, come back to the wheel every so often to see if anything has shifted. The goal is to get to a point where you are satisfied and feel like you are thriving.

WHEEL OF WORK

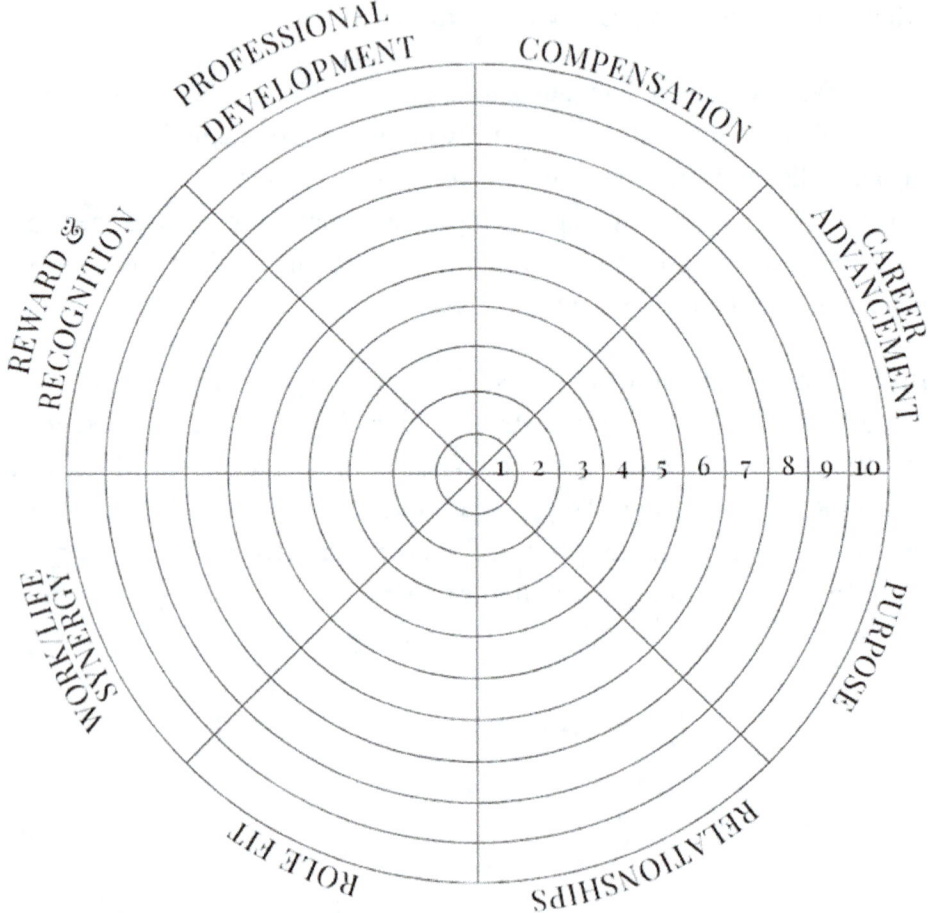

PROFESSIONAL DEVELOPMENT

COMPENSATION

REWARD & RECOGNITION

CAREER ADVANCEMENT

1 2 3 4 5 6 7 8 9 10

WORK/LIFE SYNERGY

PURPOSE

ROLE FIT

RELATIONSHIPS

Wheel of Work Reflections

Be Well to Lead Well

Chapter 1

Developing Your Psychosocial Well-Being

"The conscious choices you make every day lay the foundation for your mental and physical health and also determine the quality of life you lead."

-Sanchita Pandey

W hat does having a quality life look like? What does it mean to be a self-actualized, individuated, optimally developed, fully-well and fully-functioning human? And what does it take to become one? These are the general questions one would ask when contemplating on psychosocial well-being.

Psychosocial well-being is a concept that includes emotional or psychological well-being, as well as social and collective well-being. Psychosocial well-being is often looked at as "quality of life" because it involves emotional, social, and physical components. Having a "quality life" both inside and outside of "the office" is important. This is because our success in whatever we venture to endeavor in is tied to our ability to function at a capacity that allows us to act toward those endeavors. Call them ideas, goals, plans, or our pursuit of purpose.

Like with most other concepts and how they are applied, how psychosocial well-being is developed is determined by several factors that are complex and multivariate but crucial for us to recognize as we start to take steps toward living and working with intent, showing up as our whole selves, and having a positive impact on those with whom we cross paths. These are things we should all strive for.

To give you a little bit of history and context, the model for psychosocial well-being is underpinned by a psychological well-being model created by Carol Ryff at the University of Wisconsin-Madison. It was developed with an attempt to address the neglected aspects of positive functioning such as "purposeful engagement in life, realization of personal talents and capacities, and enlightened self-knowledge."

This endeavor sought to answer the questions:

- What constitutes the essential features of well-being?
- What are the critical components that make up the fully-well, fully-functional human?

Throughout her research, Dr. Ryff identified 6 critical components that connected the convergence of what it means to be self-actualized, individuated, fully functioning, and optimally developed; a fully-well and fully-functioning human.

Purpose in life - having goals in life and a sense of direction giving both your past and present a deeper meaning.

Autonomy - having self-determination and independence; having the ability to resist social pressures, to think and act in certain ways, and the ability to regulate your behavior from within. It means having the capability of evaluating yourself based on your personal standards.

Personal growth - having a feeling of continued development; seeing yourself as growing and expanding, being open to new experiences, and having a sense of realizing your potential. You can see improvement in yourself and your behavior over time and you change in ways that reflect more self-knowledge and effectiveness.

Environmental mastery - having the ability to control a complex array of external activities. Making effective use of your surrounding opportunities and choosing to create situations to suit your personal needs and values.

Positive relationships with others - having satisfying, trusting relationships with others; being concerned about their welfare and having strong empathy, affection, and intimacy, and understanding the give and take of human relationships.

Self-acceptance - possessing a positive attitude toward the self; you acknowledge and accept multiple aspects of yourself, including good and bad qualities, and you feel positive about your past life.

What does this look like in practice? How do we improve our psychosocial well-being and start becoming whole? How do we create a quality life?

The first step and critical starting point is to visualize the life you want. Start with your purpose. **Ask yourself:**

- Who do you want to impact?
- Why do you want to make an impact?
- How will you achieve the impact?
- What is the work that you want to do?

This may sound a bit existential, but it really is important. In order to chart a path to anywhere you have to know, at the bare minimum, the direction you want to go, and where you intend your destination to be.

The practice of becoming well and becoming whole will take a lot of work, but it is not impossible. It is an iterative process, and one we all should look forward to undertaking.

Start with visualizing the career that you want. Whether you are an entrepreneur or work for an organization, it doesn't matter. Start by identifying your purpose in the work; find the who, why, and how, and then continue on from there. Your personal standards, strategies for growth, mastering your environment, creating strategic relationships, being authentic, and showing up every day as you are most important.

Here are some Coach Yourself Questions to help you develop your psychosocial well-being.

In relation to autonomy: What are my personal standards? How will I hold true to them? How will I remain autonomous and not fall under social pressures to conform?

In relation to personal growth: What am I doing to grow and expand my horizons and realize my potential?

In relation to environmental mastery: How am I making use of my surroundings and creating situations that suit my personal needs and values?

In relation to positive relationships with others: What kind of relationships am I building and cultivating?

In relation to self-acceptance: Have I accepted myself fully? What do I love most about myself and why?

Goals for Developing Your Psychosocial Well-Being

Now, let's set some goals around developing your psychosocial well-being. Think about what you can realistically achieve in the time frame you've set for yourself. This could be over the next week, month, or several weeks. It is recommended that you identify at least three goals from the six components of psychosocial well-being.

Goal 1: _____

Goal 2: _____

Goal 3: _____

GOAL ACTION *plan*

GOAL

START: END:

. . . .

MOTIVATION

ACTION STEPS

START   COMPLETION

POSSIBLE OBSTACLES

OUTCOME

POSSIBLE SOLUTIONS

Chapter 1: Developing Your Psychosocial Well-Being   17

GOAL ACTION *plan*

GOAL

START: END:

. . . .

MOTIVATION

ACTION STEPS

START   COMPLETION

POSSIBLE OBSTACLES

OUTCOME

POSSIBLE SOLUTIONS

GOAL ACTION *plan*

GOAL

START: END:

. . . .
MOTIVATION

ACTION STEPS

START   COMPLETION

POSSIBLE OBSTACLES

OUTCOME

POSSIBLE SOLUTIONS

Be Well to Lead Well

Chapter 2

Caring for Yourself

"You yourself, as much as anybody in the entire universe, deserve your love and affection."

-Buddha

Oftentimes we forget to include ourselves when we think of love or care. We do so because it can seem selfish to think about and do for ourselves especially if we have other people in our lives. But I want to ask you this:

How often do you take care of YOU?

In this chapter, we focus on how to love and care for yourself. It may seem a bit soft and mushy, but as the saying goes, "If you can't take care of yourself how are you going to take care of others?" Or, keep in mind the other saying, "You can't pour from an empty cup."

When we think of the daily grind of work and family, the hustle and bustle of the day, we don't think about ourselves often enough. When the day is over, we head home to take care of children, parents, spouses, pets, and neglect ourselves. In order for us to be successful at being our whole selves, and bringing that whole self to work, we have to focus on loving and caring for ourselves as a forethought and not an afterthought.

No, we are not going to talk about bubble baths and lighting candles. We are going to go a bit deeper than that to discuss how to integrate self-care into your life as a practice to support your ability to show up fully present and be productive in your life and work.

So, what is love? This is an age-old question that many struggle to answer. Love can be complex, but only if one does not know what love means.

A simple, yet encompassing, definition of love is the affection, benevolence, good will, high esteem, and concern for the welfare of oneself and/or others. Did you notice?

The definition includes oneself!

Keeping in mind the definition of love, self-love is defined as the belief that you are a valuable and worthy person. Now ask yourself this; how often do you feel valuable? How often do you feel worthy?

The feelings of value and worthiness create a mindset, desire, and need to care for ourselves. Even when we feel our worst, loving ourselves allows us to recognize and move past those feelings, and to see our own value and worthiness.

So, what does self-care look like within this context?

We all face external factors that can throw a wrench into our plans. Many of them are not within our control. What is, however, is self-care. We make the choice to create space and time to engage in activities that replenish our mind, body, and spirit.

Being fully present in mind and body is a requirement for productivity in life and work. In order for us to show up fully and whole, we have to be in our best health mentally, physically, and emotionally. With all of the stressors of the world, this can be a challenge. However, it is a necessity in order for us to be happy and productive.

This is why integrating self-care as a practice is important.

There are two steps to integrating self-care as a practice. The first step is to understand what self-care looks like. Here are five examples.

Number one: Self-care is being honest. Be honest with yourself and those around you about how you are feeling.

Number two: Self-care is being kind to yourself and giving yourself some grace when you have not achieved a goal or objective.

Number three: Self-care is loving and taking care of your mind, body, and spirit and nourishing them daily.

Number four: Self-care is saying "No" when you do not have the desire or capacity to do something.

Number five: Self-care is taking breaks to rest and recalibrate.

The second part of the self-care process is identifying what's happening with you at home and at work and how those things are impacting your ability to show up fully and whole every single day. You may want to begin by taking a daily inventory of your environment.

Our environments contribute tremendously to how we feel. The energy that flows within and throughout a space impacts the energy that we receive. Our environment can be broken down into two categories. The first is our geographical location, and the second is what we would call a sub-environment, which are places like work, or home, or our car for example.

Regardless of where we are, we have to be mindful of the energy that is surrounding us. If our environment exudes negative energy, our bodies will be able to feel this in the forms of stress and anxiety.

As we all know, stress and anxiety can wreak havoc on our mind and body. We can lose sleep, we can have trouble with intimacy, we can develop aches and pains, and we can even develop chronic health issues like high blood pressure. We can withdraw socially, we can lose motivation and focus, and we can become overwhelmed.

Take a moment to take stock of your environment. **Complete these statements.**

"When at home I feel..." What is the first word that comes to mind when you think about your home environment?

Whenever I am feeling this way, I..." What action do you take to either enhance this feeling if this feeling is positive, or what action do you take to mitigate or remove the feeling if it is negative?

"When at work I feel..." What is the first word that comes to mind when you think about your work environment?

Chapter 2: Caring for Yourself

"Whenever I am feeling this way, I..." What action do you take to either enhance this feeling if this feeling is positive, or what action do you take to mitigate or remove the feeling if it is negative?

While we may not have control over all of the environments we enter, we do have control over some, and that is where we need to focus. We also have control over the energy we put into a space whether we've created the space ourselves, or are in a position to modify it. With the ultimate goal being to decrease any stress that may be present. When we think about our desire to have home and work lives where we thrive and that give us greater meaning, it is important to be aware of what needs to change for that to happen. We spend the vast majority of our time in our homes or in workspaces whether we work for ourselves or other people. During that time we want those spaces to be as stress free as possible.

Strategies for better self-care

Here are a few strategies that will help you along your self-care journey so that you are on your way to being present and productive at home and work.

Strategy number one: Face your challenges head on. Take the time to acknowledge and understand the challenges you are facing. Share them with those closest to you and ask for support when you need it.

Strategy number two: Start with a strategy, then find the techniques. Take the time to think things through. Strategize how you can address the challenges you face and then find the techniques to tackle them.

Strategy number three: Monitor yourself and take in feedback from those close with you. Pay attention to yourself, how you feel, and what you are thinking. If you feel a certain way others have probably observed it, so talk to those closest to you and ask them if they've noticed a change in you.

Be Well to Lead Well

Strategy number four: Make your environment work for you. Create spaces at home and work that energize you and allow you to thrive.

Strategy number five: Appreciate yourself, your work, and your growth. Affirm yourself daily. Schedule time to rest, relax, and recalibrate. Celebrate your accomplishments, big and small.

Here are some Coach Yourself Questions to help you develop better self-care habits

When was the last time I felt valued? When was the last time that I felt that I was desirable to myself and others?

What were some of the feelings or emotions that came along with it?

When was the last time I believed that I was deserving of all of the abundance in my life that I had sought? What were some of the other feelings and emotions that came along with it?

What is preventing me from showing up fully and wholly in my life and work?

What stressors am I currently experiencing? What are the causes of these stressors?

What can I do, or stop doing, to relieve these stressors or prevent them from reoccurring?

Goals for better self-care

Now, let's set some goals around creating better self-care habits. Think about what you can realistically achieve in the time frame you've set for yourself. This could be over the next week, month, or several weeks. It is recommended that you identify at least three goals from the five examples of self-care described earlier.

Goal 1: _____

Goal 2: _____

Goal 3: _____

GOAL ACTION *plan*

GOAL

START: **END:**

. . . .
MOTIVATION

ACTION STEPS

START   COMPLETION

POSSIBLE OBSTACLES

OUTCOME

POSSIBLE SOLUTIONS

GOAL ACTION *plan*

GOAL

START: END:

. . . .

MOTIVATION

ACTION STEPS

START   COMPLETION

POSSIBLE OBSTACLES

OUTCOME

POSSIBLE SOLUTIONS

Be Well to Lead Well

GOAL ACTION *plan*

GOAL

START: END:

MOTIVATION

ACTION STEPS

START   COMPLETION

POSSIBLE OBSTACLES

OUTCOME

POSSIBLE SOLUTIONS

Be Well to Lead Well

Chapter 3

Creating Work–Life Synergy

"Synergy is what happens when one plus one equals ten or a hundred or even a thousand! It's the profound result when two or more respectful human beings determine to go beyond their preconceived ideas to meet a great challenge."

- Stephen Covey

Work-life balance? Can it ever be achieved? It's a little more complicated than a simple yes or no. Why? Because the reality is, there will never be a time when we can devote equal amounts of time to anything in our lives. We will always be pulled in one direction that will require us to take from one area of our lives to give to another. That is why, in this chapter, the focus will be on shifting from trying to find balance between life and work to finding synergy between them.

When we think about balance what comes to mind is equal. The same amount of weight distributed on both sides of the scale. Life and work. What we often don't realize is that things happen, whether it is in our personal lives or work lives, and we get spill over. Spillover of work into home or home into work, thus throwing things off balance. The idea of having to constantly take from one area to put into another to try and achieve balance is frustrating. Balance also assumes competition of opposing sides and, with that, the requirement to put more focus on one side than the other.

So, this raises the question: does balance really exist? If it does, should we be striving for it or should we be looking for something else? Synergy perhaps?

Let's start by positing a few what-if questions.

What if we don't consider our personal lives and work lives to be in competition with one another?

What if we stop looking for ways to cut out pieces of one so that we could give to the other?

What if we shifted our minds from the concept of balance toward the idea of synergy?

Work-life synergy is the focus of finding ways that our work lives and personal lives can interact, cooperate, and create harmony out of their combined existences. In order for us to be successful at this, it requires us to make a few shifts in our thinking and doing.

Accept that life is complex. Get rid of the belief that you have to choose one aspect of your life over the other. Take the time to do an inventory of what is important to you and why.

Find common ground. Identify how the different aspects of your life are connected. Figure out how one area of your life can be helped by the other, and recognize that life is not a division between work and personal time.

Recognize that you have more than just work and personal life. Understand that there is more to you than just your personal life and work life, and discover where there is harmony. We are parents, children, siblings, friends. We have passions, and hobbies, and so much more.

Create mental boundaries for the various people, events, activities, and areas of your life. Understand how you spend your time. Are there any time suckers that you can get rid of?

Find ways to ground yourself. Engage in activities that allow you to reset so that you can have a clear mind. This includes practicing self-care and mindfulness, especially during moments of high stress and anxiety.

Take time to practice self-affirmation and reflect on your self-worth. Affirmations can help you overcome overwhelm and knowing your self-worth can help you prioritize your self-care.

Understand how your behavior contributes to your ability to be effective. Identify what behaviors add and detract from your joy and engagement.

Because we have so often seen our lives as bifurcated, making the shift from balance may be easier said than done, but it is not impossible. When we view life as having many facets the work does not seem as daunting. We also must not forget that we are more than just our individual selves and the roles we have within our organizations. Our lives don't only exist on those two planes. When we can recognize this and see how they not only all work together, but complement each other, we will be the better for it. We will find ourselves more fulfilled overall and living more harmonious lives.

Here are some Coach Yourself Questions to help you develop work-life synergy.

How do I want to spend my time? Are there ways I can plan or prioritize?

What are some of my "time suckers"? What are some things I can do to minimize time spent, but maximize impact?

What are some of my helpful habits? Can they be multiplied to prevent me from becoming overwhelmed?

How can I reclaim my time and show others how to value it?

When is the right time for me to shut down?

How can I communicate what is important to me?

How can I prioritize my work time so that it does not spill over into my leisure time?

Goals for creating work-life synergy

Now let's set some goals around creating more work-life synergy. Think about what you can realistically achieve in the time frame you've set for yourself. This could be over the next week, month, or several weeks. It is recommended that you identify at least three goals from the seven mind and action shifts described in the chapter.

Goal 1: _____

Goal 2: _____

Goal 3: _____

GOAL ACTION *plan*

GOAL

START: END:

. . . .

MOTIVATION

ACTION STEPS

START   COMPLETION

POSSIBLE OBSTACLES

OUTCOME

POSSIBLE SOLUTIONS

GOAL ACTION *plan*

GOAL

MOTIVATION

ACTION STEPS

START   COMPLETION

POSSIBLE OBSTACLES

OUTCOME

POSSIBLE SOLUTIONS

GOAL ACTION *plan*

GOAL

START: END:

. . . .

MOTIVATION

ACTION STEPS   START   COMPLETION

....

....

....

....

POSSIBLE OBSTACLES   **OUTCOME**

POSSIBLE SOLUTIONS

Be Well to Lead Well

Chapter 4

Getting Rid of
Self-Sabotaging Thoughts

"The ultimate act of surrender to God is rebellion against lies: the lies that the enemy has spoken to you, and the lies that you might have told yourself about you."

-Adrena Sawyer

The mind is incredible. It is also complex. It can take us to the most wonderful places and to the darkest. The mind is an intricate and complicated system, but possibly the most delicate tool we have as human beings. Our minds control what we think and how we behave.

When our mind is at odds with itself, our conscious mind against our subconscious mind, that is when we engage in self-sabotage.

"You did it to yourself." I'm sure you've said this to yourself on more than one occasion after you realized that what could have been a positive outcome didn't turn out the way you wanted it to because you didn't give yourself enough time to, talked yourself out of it, or even convinced yourself that you couldn't do it in the first place.

This, my friends, is self-sabotage; it can destroy you!

Self-sabotage can destroy your self-confidence, your self-esteem, and it can wreak havoc on your relationships. Self-sabotage is proving to yourself that you just couldn't do it—whatever it was, such as eating healthy, exercising more, or completing a project—or that you shouldn't have even tried.

While self-sabotage is unique to the individual and can manifest in different ways, there are three commonalities among them.

The first is procrastination - this is when you constantly put off the things you need to do, even though you know you need to finish them. You tell yourself, "I'll do it when I get back home," or "I'll do it tomorrow," or "I'll start next week." Then what happens? When you get home you say you will do it tomorrow, and when tomorrow comes you say, "I'll start next week." It is a vicious cycle that ends up with either nothing getting done, or a rushed job because a clock starts ticking. This makes the quality of whatever "it" is suffer.

The second is negative self-talk - this is when you tell yourself that you are inadequate, or unworthy of success, or engage in negative thoughts like "I can't do that!" or "I don't deserve that." Remember that time you told yourself you weren't qualified for that job, or that you didn't deserve that promotion? Those were missed opportunities that could have resulted in the exact success you were seeking when you first thought to apply for that job or contemplated asking for the promotion.

The third is the skill/will/move conflict - this is when you have the skill and the will to achieve a goal, but something keeps you from moving forward and taking the next steps. This one here is a trickster. Why? Because it takes a lot of self-reflection to determine why you didn't make that move. It is usually either procrastination or negative self-talk, but it could also be something else. Something deeper... possibly fear that is preventing you from moving, from taking a step in the direction toward achieving a goal.

Don't fear. There is light at the end of the self-sabotage tunnel. Here are three activities you can engage in to help counteract some of the effects of self-sabotage. It is not an exhaustive list, but it is definitely a place to start.

The first activity is to **develop an awareness of self-sabotaging**. We have to recognize the self-sabotaging behavior before we can work toward changing it. Engage in reflective exercises. Think about goals that you've made, but have never accomplished. Are there particular areas in your life or career that you've been putting off deciding? Do you know you have the desire and capacity to take the next step toward your goals but lack the motivation? Take the time you need to bring yourself into awareness.

The second activity is to work toward **understanding and managing the emotions that lead to self-sabotaging behaviors**. Self-sabotaging

Be Well to Lead Well

behavior is often brought on by feelings of anxiety, anger, hopelessness, or even desperation. Take the time to think about what triggered the emotion(s) you are feeling when you engage in self-sabotaging behavior. Did you have a disagreement with your spouse? Was your boss dismissive? Did a colleague receive praise for work and did not share the credit with you? When you notice that you are engaging in self-sabotaging thoughts, write them down. Do this in the moment. By monitoring your thoughts, you can better understand them, and in turn manage them.

The third activity is **developing self-supportive behaviors**. This is the opposite of self-sabotage. Self-supportive activities can help rebuild your self-esteem and shift the direction of your thoughts from can't to can. This is an active exercise rather than a reflective one, but just as important. Self-supportive behaviors can be prompted by the following questions.

- What can I say to myself that is positive or encouraging?

- What are some options that I have? Is there more than one way for me to achieve my goals?

- Can I become more confident by setting and achieving small goals on my way to achieving the bigger ones?

You may also create a thoughts habit list or table. This process will help guide you to replace self-sabotaging thoughts with self-supportive ones.

Write down your self-sabotaging thoughts. For each of those thoughts write down a self-supportive one. Repeat the self-supportive thought through rewriting it, thinking it, speaking it aloud, and reading it. Repeat that thought as many times as you need to (50 times, 100 times) every day for at least 30 days. This repetition will cause a new habit of self-supportive behavior and begin to replace the negative thoughts with positive ones.

It is common knowledge that as human beings we tend to focus on the negative more than the positive. Challenge yourself to change that narrative. Move from self-sabotage to self-support and begin to create the outcomes you desire.

Healthy Thought Habits

Completing a Healthy Thought Habits table is an exercise in awareness. Taking note of your goals and the thoughts you have around them are very important. Using this guide, you will begin to start replacing self-sabotaging thoughts that prevent you from achieving your goals with self-supportive ones to help you achieve them. Research has shown that it takes approximately 60 days to form a new habit. You've got goals to achieve so lets get started!

Choose a goal.

Identify a self-sabotaging thought you've had about the goal.

Replace the self-sabotaging thought with a self-supportive one.

Repeat the self-supportive thought through writing, thinking, and speaking it multiple times a day for the next 60 days.

Document your progress for each goal.

GOAL	SELF-SABOTAGING THOUGHTS	SELF-SUPPORTIVE THOUGHTS

Thought Habits Progress Notes

Here are some Coach Yourself Questions to help you remove self-sabotaging thoughts.

Is there anything that I need to finish that I am putting off?

What are some of the negative thoughts I've been having around these tasks/goals?

What is one positive thought I can associate with these tasks/goals?

Are there tasks/goals I have wanted to do that I have convinced myself I either can't or am not worthy of?

What are some of the experiences I've had around completing/achieving those tasks/goals that have made me believe I'm unworthy?

What have I not been able to move forward on even though I know it is something that I both want and am capable of doing or achieving? What is one step I can take in the next day, week, or month to achieve these goals?

Goals for getting rid of self-sabotaging thoughts

Now let's set some goals around removing self-sabotaging thoughts so that you can achieve all the goals you set for yourself. Think about what you can realistically achieve in the time frame you've set for yourself. This could be over the next week, month, or several weeks. It is recommended that you identify at least one goal for each of the three ways self-sabotage manifests.

Goal 1: _____

Goal 2: _____

Goal 3: _____

GOAL ACTION *plan*

GOAL

START: END:

. . . .

MOTIVATION

ACTION STEPS

START   COMPLETION

. . . .

. . . .

. . . .

. . . .

POSSIBLE OBSTACLES

OUTCOME

POSSIBLE SOLUTIONS

GOAL ACTION *plan*

GOAL

. . . .

MOTIVATION

ACTION STEPS

START   COMPLETION

....

....

....

....

POSSIBLE OBSTACLES

OUTCOME

POSSIBLE SOLUTIONS

Be Well to Lead Well

GOAL ACTION *plan*

GOAL

START: END:

. . . .

MOTIVATION

ACTION STEPS

START   COMPLETION

POSSIBLE OBSTACLES

OUTCOME

POSSIBLE SOLUTIONS

Chapter 4: Getting Rid of Self-Sabotaging Thoughts   61

Be Well to Lead Well

Chapter 5

Creating a Personal Mission

"A small body of determined spirits fired by an unquenchable faith in their mission can alter the course of history."

— Mahatma Gandhi

Be Well to Lead Well

We all strive to stand for something greater than ourselves, right? We all want to have a purpose in life. For some of us, it is easy to identify what that means is, while others may find It more challenging. Having a personal mission statement, however, can help guide us in the direction of discovering who we are. It provides us with a roadmap as we navigate life and work, and does so with intent and purpose.

So, what is a personal mission statement?

It is a statement that (1) defines your values, (2) defines who you are as a person or a professional, (3) identifies what your goals are, and (4) identifies how you define your success.

Creating a personal mission statement is a multi-step process, and it requires active reflection.

The first step is to identify past successes. We often get stuck in the rut of everyday life and work and neglect to take the time to reflect on what we have accomplished.

Take some time and ask yourself...

What have I accomplished in the past that I am proud of?

For some of us, it can be challenging to identify what goals we have achieved. This is because, oftentimes, we are just doing. We don't take the time to stop and think about the nuances and the impact. However, when you think about past successes, goals you have accomplished in the past that you are most proud of, you will begin to rewire your brain to focus on and gravitate toward the positive.

The second step is identifying your core values. Ask yourself...

What are the qualities that you believe identify who you are and what you believe in? What is most important to you right now to live your best life or create a career where you can thrive? When thinking about core values, it might be best to start off with thinking about values for your life. These are considered foundational and they often carry over into the values you have related to your work. Your foundational values will always impact the work you do.

The third step is to identify what you would like to contribute. This can be to your life, family, community, or organization. Ask yourself...

What can I do that will make a positive impact on my life and the lives of others? These can be family, friends, community, or organization, as stated before. Your personal mission goes beyond you as the individual because it will impact everyone around you. Make a list of what they are.

The fourth step is identifying your goals. Think about what is important for you and what you would like to accomplish personally and by when. Write down your short term and long-term goals. Make them SMART goals: Specific, Measurable, Attainable, Realistic, and Time bound. Do the same for your professional goals. What would you like to accomplish professionally and by when?

The last step is creating the statement.

A personal mission statement can guide you in every aspect of your life. It keeps you on track to creating the abundance and success you desire. It is a reminder of who you are, and who you strive to be. Once you write your mission statement, carry it with you. Take it out every once in a while and read it. Remind yourself of who you are, what you aim to achieve, and the value that you bring to the world.

Here is an example of a mission statement.

My mission is to create a life for me and my family that is filled with joy, gratitude, laughter, and abundance. **I will achieve this through** consistently working on my purpose, not placing any limitations on myself, and continuously creating spaces **where I**, and others, can connect and learn from one another and collectively thrive in our homes and in the work that we do.

Your mission statement should start with "My mission is". It should identify what you would like to achieve and how you will achieve it. "I will achieve this through". Lastly, it should state the impact you want to make or the change you would like to see: "where I".

Creating a personal mission statement is not a one and done exercise. You will find yourself revising it several times over as your life's circumstances change. Your personal mission may change as you change jobs, or if there are major life changes like building a family. The goal is to always have one to guide you.

Here are some Coach Yourself Questions to help you identify your personal mission and develop a mission statement:

The world that I want to live in; what does it look like?

What are my personal beliefs?

What excites me about life and gets me out of bed in the mornings?

What is my purpose and meaning in life?

What motivates and energizes me?

What impact and change do I want to have on the world?

What would I like to contribute to others, and how will I do so?

Now, let's create a mission Statement!

Using the Coach Yourself Questions as your guide, complete the worksheet to develop your personal mission statement.

My Personal Mission Statement

Using the "coach yourself" questions as your guide, complete the worksheet to develop your personal mission statement.

What are my past successes?	
What are my core values?	
What would I like to contribute to my life/work?	
My Goals	
My Mission Statement	

Notes

Be Well to Lead Well

Chapter 6

Strengthening Your Self-Efficacy

"In order to succeed, people need a sense of self-efficacy, to struggle together with resilience to meet the inevitable obstacles and inequities of life.

— Alfred Bandura

Do you believe that you can be successful? Do you believe that you can achieve anything you set your mind to? Do you believe that you can overcome any challenge placed in front of you? If you answered yes, kudos, you are one self-efficacious individual.

Not everyone has a high level of belief in themselves. In fact, most people don't. The good news is that, for those of us who don't always believe in our ability to push through and reach our goals, we can strengthen our self-efficacy and invite abundance and success into our lives.

What is fundamental to our ability to engage in any activity is the motivation we have based on what we believe to be our likelihood of success in that endeavor.

This is our self-efficacy. It is the probability we estimate that we can take on any task before us. For example, the probability that you, as a leader, can motivate your team to accomplish a task, or your ability to motivate them to solve problems in new ways. It is your belief in your ability to achieve a goal you set for yourself.

Self-efficacy is what motivates us to choose and welcome challenges, and to use our strengths and skills to meet those challenges.

Self-efficacy encourages and energizes us to pursue our goals and invest in the time and effort needed to accomplish them. It helps us persevere when we are presented with obstacles that would otherwise force us to throw in the towel.

Research has shown that our levels of self-efficacy are impacted by four processes.

The first is the Cognitive Process. This is how our thoughts shape our reality.

The second is the Motivational Process. These are our beliefs regarding how expected outcomes may shape our motivation to move forward.

The third is the Affective Process. This explains how our ability to cope determines whether or not we decide to avoid a situation.

The fourth is the Selection Process. These are our choices on what situations we expose ourselves to, based on our belief of whether we can master it or not.

Self Efficacy Self Reflection

Take a moment to think about an area of your life that you feel very confident about. This can be work, family, a relationship, school, a friendship, or a hobby.

Note all of the various tasks you need to perform in this area of your life in order for you to feel like it is successful. Now prioritize the list. Identify the most important three or four tasks that impact your overall success and on a scale of one to one hundred (1-100), determine how confident you are that you can do the following three things;

1. At least get by on these tasks.

2. Meet your own and others expectations in performing these tasks.

3. Excel in accomplishing these tasks.

Area of Life:

TASK	CONFIDENCE LEVEL
	I can at least get by on this task. _____ I can meet my own and others expectations in performing this task. _____ I can excel in accomplishing these tasks. _____
	I can at least get by on this task. _____ I can meet my own and others expectations in performing this task. _____ I can excel in accomplishing these tasks. _____
	I can at least get by on this task. _____ I can meet my own and others expectations in performing this task. _____ I can excel in accomplishing these tasks. _____
	I can at least get by on this task. _____ I can meet my own and others expectations in performing this task. _____ I can excel in accomplishing these tasks. _____

As you work through this exercise, you will notice that your level of self-efficacy will vary depending on which area of your life you are assessing. You will also realize that no matter how confident you are in one area of your life, you can be equally unsure in others. Other things to also make note of:

- You find yourself most confident in the things that you have done repeatedly and have mastered.

- How others perceive your ability will impact your belief in your own.

- When you need resources to complete a task or goal, whether or not you have access to them will also play a role in your level of efficacy.

So, if you are running low in the self-efficacy department, what should you do? Here are four ways that you can strengthen your self-efficacy.

Focus on past success: Look at past success. This is a robust way to increase levels of self-efficacy. In any environment, it is often helpful to appreciate previous success stories rather than creating new ones.

Model others: Seeing people who are in similar situations overcome obstacles increases the belief that one, too, can do it. What's important though, is that the models need to be perceived as similar enough to oneself in order to feel a strong sense of confidence in one's capabilities.

Create situations for success: While verbal persuasion can be a great source of confidence, it can be difficult to overcome self-doubts. In addition to telling yourself that you can do something, structure situations that bring success. Avoid placing yourself into situations, prematurely, where you are likely to fail.

Reframe negative experiences: The ways in which we interpret our physical and emotional reactions to stressful or tense situations affect how we judge our vulnerability and fatigue in regards to stress. People with high levels of self-efficacy are able to recognize a state of affective arousal as an energizing facilitator of performance.

Self-efficacy is about conviction; it is about our ability to activate the motivation, resources, and actions needed to be successful at executing tasks and achieving the goals we set for ourselves.

When we have high self-efficacy, we invite abundance into our lives and, in turn, achieve success.

Individuals with high self-efficacy, regardless whether it is in their personal or work lives, individuals with high self-efficacy recognize success and have the following five things in common:

They set high goals for themselves and have the capability of self-selecting in difficult situations.

- They welcome and thrive on challenges.
- They are highly self-motivated.
- They invest in the necessary effort to accomplish their goals.
- When faced with obstacles, they persevere.

The moral of the story is **if you believe it, you can achieve it!** It may sound a bit cliche, but it is true. Believing that we can accomplish a goal motivates us to get up, do the work, face the challenges as they come, and achieve what we set out to do.

Here are some Coach Yourself Questions to help you strengthen your self-efficacy.

What accomplishments am I most proud of and why?

What challenges have I overcome that I initially thought I could not get through?

What was one of the most recent challenges I've faced, and how can I transform that experience into a positive lesson and an opportunity for growth?

What type of confidence would I like to have, and do I know anyone who has it that I can model?

What was the best moment of my...

day?

week?

month?

year?

Goals for strengthening your self-efficacy

Now let's set some goals around strengthening your self-efficacy. Think about what you can realistically achieve in the time frame you've set for yourself. This could be over the next week, month, or several weeks. It is recommended that you identify at least one goal for each of the four ways you can strengthen your self-efficacy.

Goal 1: _____

Goal 2: _____

Goal 3: _____

Goal 4: _____

GOAL ACTION *plan*

GOAL

START: END:

. . . .

MOTIVATION

ACTION STEPS

START   COMPLETION

POSSIBLE OBSTACLES

OUTCOME

POSSIBLE SOLUTIONS

GOAL ACTION *plan*

GOAL

START: END:

. . . .

MOTIVATION

ACTION STEPS

START   COMPLETION

....

....

....

....

POSSIBLE OBSTACLES

OUTCOME

POSSIBLE SOLUTIONS

GOAL ACTION *plan*

GOAL

START: END:

. . . .
MOTIVATION

ACTION STEPS

START   COMPLETION

POSSIBLE OBSTACLES

OUTCOME

POSSIBLE SOLUTIONS

GOAL ACTION *plan*

GOAL

START: END:

. . . .

MOTIVATION

ACTION STEPS

START   COMPLETION

POSSIBLE OBSTACLES

OUTCOME

POSSIBLE SOLUTIONS

Chapter 7

Recognizing Your Strengths

"**Success is achieved by developing your strengths, not by eliminating your weaknesses.**"

— Marilyn vos Savant

All of us have talents, skills, or strengths that we either don't recognize or take for granted. Sometimes we may take them for granted because they seem to just be a part of who we are. We've always had them, they come easy, or they seem common. We tend not to recognize them because we may not have opportunities to use them frequently enough to even notice that they exist.

Gallup defines strengths as "those activities for which one can provide consistent, near-perfect performance. Strengths are composed of skills, knowledge and talent."

Our strengths can be particular ways in which we do things, how we process information, or ability to strategize or empathize. Our strengths inform how we think about ourselves, how we interact with others, and the opportunities we have to make an impact on our lives and work.

In order for us to really maximize our strengths, we have to first identify what they are.

Once you've identified what your strengths are, the next step is to focus on them. It is so much easier to get bogged down with the things we aren't as strong because they take far less energy to think about. However, working on our strengths, even if it requires more effort, will allow us to reach our goals and attain the success we are looking for more quickly and with greater impact.

So where should you begin? Here are three strategies to help you focus on and work on your strengths to be more efficient, effective, and productive to make a greater impact?

Strategy # 1: Identify, name, and concentrate on your strengths. Identify what makes you unique, valuable, and passionate about your life and career. Talk to your family, colleagues, friends. Ask them what they see. There are also several assessments that you can take to help you discover your strengths. When you concentrate on your strengths you will feel a greater sense of fulfillment and forward progress toward your goals.

Strategy #2: Don't compare yourself to others. While some of our strengths may not be unique to us, how we apply them and the impact they leave is. This does not mean that you should not engage others and learn from them. Consider allying yourself with people you may feel are your competitors, and open yourself up to learning from them. You may discover new things about yourself.

Strategy #3: Surround yourself with people whose strengths complement yours. You cannot be an expert at everything, so surround yourself with others who have the know-how about things you don't. Learn from them. Capitalize on the strengths of others and use the experience of working with them as an opportunity for observation and personal progress.

According to Gallup research, working in your strengths can lead to improved health and wellness, higher engagement, and overall happier lives.

Recognizing your strengths and working in them every day will help you grow, develop, and succeed. Who doesn't want that?

Here are some Coach Yourself Questions to help you recognize and work in your strengths.

What kinds of activities am I naturally drawn to?

What activities energize me?

What activities do I engage in that I feel are frustrating or draining?

What are some activities I seem to pick up quickly?

What kinds of activities take me longer to master even when I know all of the steps?

What activities have I succeeded in and thought to myself, "How did I do that?"

What activities have I enjoyed doing and while engaged in them thought to myself "When can I do them again?"

Goals for recognizing your strengths

Now, let's set some goals around recognizing your strengths. Think about what you can realistically achieve in the time frame you've set for yourself. This could be over the next week, month, or several weeks. It is recommended that you identify at least one goal for each of the strategies described in the chapter.

Goal 1: _____

Goal 2: _____

Goal 3: _____

GOAL ACTION *plan*

GOAL

START: END:

. . . .
MOTIVATION

ACTION STEPS

START   COMPLETION

....

....

....

....

POSSIBLE OBSTACLES

OUTCOME

POSSIBLE SOLUTIONS

GOAL ACTION *plan*

GOAL

START: END:

. . . .

MOTIVATION

ACTION STEPS

START   COMPLETION

....

....

....

....

POSSIBLE OBSTACLES

OUTCOME

POSSIBLE SOLUTIONS

GOAL ACTION *plan*

GOAL

START: END:
. . . .
MOTIVATION

ACTION STEPS

START   COMPLETION

POSSIBLE OBSTACLES

OUTCOME

POSSIBLE SOLUTIONS

Be Well to Lead Well

Chapter 8

Building Resilience

"It's your reaction to adversity, not adversity itself that determines how your life's story will develop."

— Dieter F. Uchtdorf

Be Well to Lead Well

It is not often that we consider resilience as a cornerstone for productivity and success in the workplace. However, research has shown that resilience has profound implications for promoting competence and human capital in individuals and society. Having the ability to bounce back from difficulties, whether they be environmental situations or people related, is critical for our ability to be and stay productive and be active participants in our lives, families, and careers.

We will face challenges wherever we are and wherever we go, but it is our resilience that will allow us to keep our head up and move forward in spite of it all.

As it is defined, resilience is the capacity to rebound from adversity, conflict, failure or even positive events, progress, and increased responsibility. These are all things we encounter every day at home and at work. It is our resilience, though, that allows us to bounce back, be renewed, and ready for what lies ahead of us.

As we begin to think about what resilience means for us as we prepare to start a new day, new project, or new role, it is important for us to be able to sit and reflect on our experiences with adversity, conflict, failure, and even positive events that seemed overwhelming. The key is to determine whether or not you have bounced back from that challenge and, if so, identify how so that you can keep those strategies with you to employ them again.

When you may not have bounced back, but felt diminished or depleted, think about someone you know and have deep respect for, such as a leader or mentor who has overcome challenges or adversity, and recognize what you can learn from them. What can you learn from their resilience that you can apply to your own development?

There are three key skills that help us develop stronger resilience and move us into the headspace we will need to help us bounce back and leap forward.

The first is emotional intelligence. Emotional intelligence has been shown to be extremely useful for individuals who frequently experience difficulties in the workplace. Being able to regulate and manage our emotions allows us to make rational decisions which lead to more positive outcomes than emotional decisions.

The second is authenticity. Having a personal sense of self and connecting it with how you express yourself on the outside allows for can't be our authentic selves. When we feel like we can't be our authentic selves and work to our strengths, that affects our perception of our ability to successfully overcome a difficult situation.

The third is agility. This is our ability to transform obstacles into opportunities, quickly. When we are agile, we are able to think and understand in the moment how we can, should, or need to pivot and shift the directions to control the outcome.

Being resilient is more than just coping during difficult times. Being resilient is proactive, and it can lead to positive and sustainable performance. When you have the capacity to overcome, steer through, bounce back, and reach out in pursuit of knowledge, experience, and creating deeper relationships with others, you are able to find so much more meaning in your life and work.

Here are some Coach Yourself Questions to help you build resilience.

What was a recent event or situation where I felt overwhelmed?

Was the overwhelm sudden and unexpected, or gradual and emotionally draining?

What were some of the coping strategies I used? Were any of those strategies effective?

Was I able to bounce back from this situation? Have I fully recovered?

What are some of the lessons I learned from this experience?
In hindsight, do I believe that I have grown or matured, bounced back to normal or beyond, or do I feel I've deteriorated or diminished?

Who do I know that has experienced the same type of situation, and how did they overcome it?

What can I learn from their resilience that I can apply to my own development?

Goals for building resilience

Now, let's set some goals around building resilience. Think about what you can realistically achieve in the time frame you've set for yourself. This could be over the next week, month, or several weeks. It is recommended that you identify at least one goal for each of the three skills for developing stronger resilience described in the chapter.

Goal 1: _____

Goal 2: _____

Goal 3: _____

GOAL ACTION *plan*

GOAL

START: END:

. . . .

MOTIVATION

ACTION STEPS

START   COMPLETION

....

....

....

....

POSSIBLE OBSTACLES

OUTCOME

POSSIBLE SOLUTIONS

Be Well to Lead Well

GOAL ACTION *plan*

GOAL

START: END:

. . . .
MOTIVATION

ACTION STEPS

START   COMPLETION

....

....

....

....

POSSIBLE OBSTACLES

OUTCOME

POSSIBLE SOLUTIONS

Chapter 8: Building Resilience   107

GOAL ACTION *plan*

GOAL

START: END:

. . . .

MOTIVATION

ACTION STEPS

START   COMPLETION

POSSIBLE OBSTACLES

OUTCOME

POSSIBLE SOLUTIONS

Be Well to Lead Well

Chapter 9

Overcoming Overwhelm

"You may not control all the events that happen to you, but you can decide not to be reduced by them."

— Maya Angelou

We all can get overwhelmed at work. The demands we place on ourselves, compounded with those placed on us by our managers and teams, can cause stress, anxiety, and overwhelm.

When we begin to feel these things, it is important for us to recognize them as soon as possible, and act to prevent them from overpowering our will and capacity to perform.

While it's best to remove ourselves from environments that cause us stress, anxiety, and overwhelm, it can be hard to do when we're in the middle of work.

Being constantly overwhelmed can impact you in several ways. These include difficulty concentrating, forgetfulness, confusion, difficulty problem solving, and even mental slowness. This can be brought on by having too many demands, overextending ourselves, or not taking the time to rest. When we are overwhelmed, we can get fatigued which can result in distractions, lack of motivation, and even more overwhelm.

One way to prevent yourself from becoming overwhelmed, or at least help you become less overwhelmed, is to figure out how to calm yourself within the moment. It is important to take the time to stop, even for a minute, to recalibrate your emotional response and to bring yourself to a place where you can either respond thoughtfully or continue to be productive.

The first step is to recognize whether whatever is causing the overwhelm is within your control. Overwhelm is good at creating a sense of helplessness. Focusing on what you are able to control can help reduce the feeling of overwhelm.

Now that you have recognized what is outside of your control, the next step is to determine whether or not you can accept that it is out of your control. Making a conscious effort to let go of the things you can't control helps reduce the stress and anxiety that often accompany the feeling of being overwhelmed.

Chapter 9: Building Resilience

The act of self-reflection can take some time, and you may need something to do in the moment to help you overcome the overwhelm you are feeling. Research has shown that one of the best ways to overcome overwhelm is to practice mindfulness. The easiest and least time-consuming ways are to recite mantras or affirmations. You can do this at your desk, on the way to a meeting, or even after a meeting to help you get into a better headspace.

Here are 10 affirmations that you can recite to yourself when you feel overwhelmed at work. They may help you to relax and relieve your mind before entering into stressful work situations.

10 Affirmations To Recite When You Feel Overwhelmed at Work

I am calm and confident.

I am worthy of being in every room I enter, in every seat I take, and at every table I sit.

My health and wellbeing are more important than anything else.

When I engage in positive thoughts and behaviors, the results I get will be positive.

I define who I am and will not allow anyone to create my story.

I chose to share my time, space, and energy with people who invest in my success.

I choose to focus my energy on people and activities that motivate me toward achieving my goals.

I choose peace and prosperity over conflicts and hardships.

I am only in control of my own thoughts, actions, and behaviors.

The things that I do not succeed at are not failures, they are opportunities for me to learn.

Be Well to Lead Well

Here are some Coach Yourself Questions to help you overcome overwhelm.

What are the things in my life/work that are currently causing me stress?

How has this stress manifested for me? What part of the situation is within my control to change?

Have I experienced this type of stress before, and what did I do in the past to overcome it?

What are some things in my life/work that I can change to ease the amount of overwhelm I am feeling?

What are some steps I can take to work through my stress and anxiety to overcome overwhelm?

Goals for overcoming overwhelm

Now, let's set some goals around overcoming overwhelm. Think about what you can realistically achieve in the time frame you've set for yourself. This could be over the next week, month, or several weeks. It is recommended that you identify at least one for preventing or minimizing overwhelm in your life.

Goal 1: _____

GOAL ACTION *plan*

GOAL

START: END:

. . . .

MOTIVATION

ACTION STEPS

START   COMPLETION

POSSIBLE OBSTACLES

OUTCOME

POSSIBLE SOLUTIONS

Be Well to Lead Well

Chapter 10

Achieving Flow

"Creating meaning involves bringing order to the contents of the mind by integrating one's actions into a unified flow experience."

- Mihaly Csikszentmihalyi

What is flow? Related to concepts like happiness and optimal experience, flow, according to some of the founders of the positive psychology movement, is a state that is attained when someone has both high skills and is undergoing significant challenges. Being in flow, which is described as a kind of euphoria, is a feeling that many experience but few can really describe or comprehend. It is the holistic experience that people feel when they act with total involvement.

To be quite honest, it is not easy to achieve a state of flow. Flow involves a deeper perspective than, let's say, general intrinsic motivation to get things done.

When someone is in flow, accomplishing goals becomes the greater reward as an end in itself rather than a means toward other goals.

There are five overarching concepts of flow.

- Happiness, optimal experience, and flow are related. These are all positive, which tells us that being in flow is beneficial to our well-being. Specifically, our subjective well-being.

- Flow is a state, which means it is something you can move in and out of. This tells us that we have some level of control over our ability to be in flow.

- To attain flow, you must have high skills and be undergoing significant challenges at the same time. Challenge does not equal difficulty. For example, it can be a challenge to attain a goal.

- Flow, which is likened to euphoria, is not an uncommon experience, but is difficult to describe or comprehend. This is because the process of flow is subconscious. While we become aware of being in this state after we come out of it, we generally aren't aware of being in flow while we are in it.

- Flow is deeper than general intrinsic motivations. It is when the work that goes into achieving the end goal is more rewarding than the actual end goal itself.

Science has shown that flow takes place when you experience a challenge in a specific situation, and that experience is balanced with your perceived abilities and skills to meet the demands of that challenge. This may sound complicated, but that's because it is.

What that means is that when a challenge exceeds your perceived skills, the resulting anxiety and diminished self-efficacy will impede your engagement, enjoyment, motivation, and, thus, your flow. Conversely, when a challenge is proven to be below your skill level, boredom and apathy will take your attention away from the activity and will cause you to lose flow.

So, what does it take to achieve flow? There are three things that need to happen.

Number one: In order to be in flow, your experience of an opportunity or challenge has to be balanced with your perceived ability to meet the challenge or take advantage of the opportunity. This means that the challenge you are being faced with has to be equal to your level of skill to meet the challenge and work through it.

Number two: If the challenge is greater than your belief in your ability to meet it, you will experience anxiety and a diminished belief in your ability to meet that challenge. These, in turn, result in low engagement, low enjoyment, and low motivation to engage in any activities that will help you to meet the challenge.

Number three: If you believe that a task is beneath your level of skill, you will get bored, you will lose focus and, therefore, will not be able to reach a state of flow to accomplish the task.

So, why should you want to achieve flow?

- Being in flow results in positive outcomes.

- Flow has been shown to have a positive correlation to academic, artistic, literary, and sports performance, as well as physical and psychosocial health. This illustrates the connection between flow and success across the board.

- Being in flow allows us to achieve far more than we could if we were out of it, or have never experienced flow, which many people haven't.

Here are five suggestions on how to achieve flow.

- Identify your distractions and eliminate them.

- Review the challenges and opportunities associated with attaining your goals and your thoughts and feelings about your ability to meet those challenges and opportunities.

- Continuously set new goals and open yourself to experiences and environments that will result in an evolution of flow.

- Actively work on increasing your knowledge, skills, abilities, and other attributes to position yourself to meet the growing complexities of the challenges, opportunities, and environments you encounter as you rise to higher levels in your work and craft.

- Give yourself the space and time to take a break, rest, and recalibrate so that when you are ready to start again, you can get into your flow.

When we think about flow in relation to our levels of performance, either how we perform within our roles in an organization, or performance within our own business as an entrepreneur or content creator, there are three questions we should reflect on.

Question one: What am I doing when I experience flow and tell myself "I got this!" and am able to complete task after task?

Question two: What am I doing when I feel too overwhelmed to focus on getting started or finishing a task or activity?

Question three: Which tasks do I perform that bore me? These are the ones that make me say, "I hate doing this," or they result in doing something other than what I need to do.

These varying feelings toward your work, tasks, challenges, or opportunities in regard to your ability or inability to be in flow are direct results of the balance between what needs to be achieved and your belief in your ability to achieve it.

Research suggests that working in your strengths can increase your flow. When you are able to concentrate on your strengths, you are more engaged, and the results are greater performance and fulfillment.

When you work in your strengths, the perception of the work shifts and enhances your experience of flow. It's the concept many talk about as being the difference in our levels of enjoyment when performing tasks that we do not see as "work."

As we aim to achieve flow so that we may not only improve our overall performance, and also our overall productivity, it is important for us to identify the distractions that prevent us from experiencing flow. When we are aware of what distracts us, it becomes easier for us to refocus, and therefore achieve flow.

There are three types of distractions to look out for.

The first are physical distractions - These include those that impact your senses like noise, lighting, or room temperature. We may not really think about these things and the impact they have on our ability to focus and reach a state of flow. Whenever you enter your work environment, at home or in the office, take an inventory of your environment.

The second are social distractions - These include conflicts, power struggles, distrust, and lack of transparency, and cause your attention to focus on defensive behavior rather than an openness to the changing environment; this contributes to evolving stages of flow. Take some time to identify some of the social distractions you may be facing in your workplace.

The third are emotional distractions - These include feelings of guilt, disengagement, or burnout from long hours of work. All of this impacts the work-life alignment that is necessary for achieving optimal well-being in every aspect of our lives.

When we think about our ability to accomplish anything we set our hearts and minds to achieve, and when we embark on the journey to do the necessary work, it is in being in flow that gives us those feelings of happiness, elation, euphoria, and overcoming.

Here are some Coach Yourself Questions to help you achieve flow.

Is my physical environment conducive to achieving my goals and the associated activities? What are some things I can do to change my environment to support my desire to achieve flow?

Does my workspace allow me to focus on my tasks and reach a state of flow? What are some of the things I can change about my workspace to help me achieve flow?

Am I experiencing conflicts that impact my ability to focus on achieving my goals? With whom? Where are the conflicts stemming from?

Are there any things happening in my social spaces that are preventing me from focusing on achieving my goals? What can I do to change the circumstances to support my goals?

Am I experiencing any emotional distractions that are preventing me from achieving my goals? What are some activities I can engage in to achieve optimal well-being?

Goals for achieving flow

Now let's set some goals around achieving flow. Think about what you can realistically achieve in the time frame you've set for yourself. This could be over the next week, month, or several weeks. It is recommended that you identify at least one goal for removing each of the distractions that prevent flow described in the chapter.

Goal 1: _____

Goal 2: _____

Goal 3: _____

GOAL ACTION *plan*

GOAL

START: END:

. . . .

MOTIVATION

ACTION STEPS

START   COMPLETION

POSSIBLE OBSTACLES

OUTCOME

POSSIBLE SOLUTIONS

Be Well to Lead Well

GOAL ACTION *plan*

GOAL

START: END:

. . . .

MOTIVATION

ACTION STEPS

START   COMPLETION

....

....

....

POSSIBLE OBSTACLES

OUTCOME

POSSIBLE SOLUTIONS

GOAL ACTION *plan*

GOAL

START: END:

. . . .

MOTIVATION

ACTION STEPS   START   COMPLETION

....

....

....

....

POSSIBLE OBSTACLES

OUTCOME

POSSIBLE SOLUTIONS

Be Well to Lead Well

Chapter 11

Managing Yourself Through Change

"The only way to make sense out of change is to plunge into it, move with it, and join the dance."

— Alan Watts

Change can be scary. It can even be traumatic if it is unexpected. However, change is ever constant. It is the one thing we can count on to always occur, and it is the one thing we can almost guarantee will leave an impact on us. Whether that impact is big or small, it is up to us to adjust to, adapt to, and accept that change and anticipate more change to come.

While we cannot change the fact that we will be impacted by change, how we are impacted is variable, and it is something that we can control.

Many of us are creatures of habit. Our routines and rituals give us comfort and feelings of safety and security, so when any of those things gets interrupted, or are changed, it can seem extremely challenging to regain a sense of normalcy.

So how do we overcome that challenge and control how change and unanticipated interruptions impact our lives impact?

We normalize change. We adjust as needed and make it a part of our lives.

We can all identify so many changes that have happened in our lives, whether they are personal or professional. In some cases, for some of us, change happens almost daily.

Knowing that change is bound to happen, there is really only one thing we can do to keep ourselves from being overwhelmed by it; that's to anticipate it. It is having a general expectation that change will happen, that we can prepare ourselves mentally and emotionally to deal with it.

When we can anticipate change, we are better able to implement the three A's to managing change.

Adjusting to it: Adjusting to change is the ability to make a shift, sometimes in the moment, to lessen the impact on your ability to function. It is about being agile and resilient so that we are prepared to face the change head on.

Adapting to it: Adapting to change means understanding what you need to do to continue to be as present and productive as possible in order to meet the new demands has placed on you. Do you need to upskill, reskill, add to, or let go of something to live and work within the change effectively?

Accepting it: Accepting change is just that. Understanding that the change that has occurred is something that was supposed to happen, seeing it for what it is, acknowledging the impact it has had on you, and letting go of any negative feelings you have about it. Yes, your feelings are real and valid, but there is no need to sit in them for any longer than is needed.

All of us have experienced change. We've experienced loss. We've experienced gain. We've experienced drastic events. We've experienced minor ones. In each of these scenarios, and others, we've reacted, been impacted, adjusted, adapted to it, and accepted it.

Using these past experiences and reflecting on how we were able to manage ourselves through them will enable us to manage ourselves through new change.

While there is no way to predict when change will occur, and what that change will be, we can prepare ourselves by knowing and understanding that at some point it will.

By normalizing change and accepting that we cannot control it, we may fear it less, and even welcome it.

Here are some Coach Yourself Questions to help you manage yourself through change.

What was my most recent experience with a major change in my life or work?

How was I impacted by that change? Was the impact positive or negative?

What was my reaction to that change? Did I react positively or negatively?

What kind of adjustments did I need to make because of this change?

Was I able to adapt to the change?

Was I able to accept the change?

Was this change something that I could have anticipated?

What was the upside to the change? What positive outcomes did this change create in my life/career?

Be Well to Lead Well

Goals for managing yourself through change

Now let's set some goals around managing yourself through change. Think about what you can realistically achieve in the time frame you've set for yourself. This could be over the next week, month, or several weeks. It is recommended that you identify at least one goal for each of the three ways to manage change described in the chapter.

Goal 1: _____

Goal 2: _____

Goal 3: _____

GOAL ACTION *plan*

GOAL

START: END:

. . . .

MOTIVATION

ACTION STEPS

START   COMPLETION

POSSIBLE OBSTACLES

OUTCOME

POSSIBLE SOLUTIONS

GOAL ACTION *plan*

GOAL

START: END:

. . . .

MOTIVATION

ACTION STEPS

        START   COMPLETION

POSSIBLE OBSTACLES

OUTCOME

POSSIBLE SOLUTIONS

GOAL ACTION *plan*

GOAL

START: END:

. . . .
MOTIVATION

ACTION STEPS   START   COMPLETION

....

....

....

....

POSSIBLE OBSTACLES

OUTCOME

POSSIBLE SOLUTIONS

Chapter 12

Building Positive Relationships

"We can improve our relationships with others by leaps and bounds if we become encouragers instead of critics"

— Joyce Meyer

Science says that our brains are hardwired to connect. We have neural networks that promote social connection and help us build relationships. When our relationships are positive and healthy, we can experience several positive outcomes, including:

- experiencing less stress
- healing faster from trauma
- living overall healthier lives
- having a greater sense of purpose
- living longer

Building relationships and making the right connections can have a huge impact on career advancing opportunities. There are some of us who are naturals at human connection, and there are others who may find it a bit challenging. When we find it difficult to connect with people, we may engage in counterproductive behaviors like isolating ourselves, but it is important to understand why it is important to create relationships.

As humans, it is natural for us to want to be recognized by those around us. Whether it be by friends, family, or colleagues, recognition of our existence shows the value that we hold as individuals. When we feel like we are not "seen" or acknowledged by others, we can become stressed and anxious, and both of those can prevent us from being fully present. Research has shown that when we feel a sense of connection, not only does it improve our mental health, but it can also inspire us to seek out experiences we may have once been afraid to because we did not want to do it alone. According to psychological research, feeling connected to others is a basic human need. Having positive relationships impacts our physical, mental, and emotional health, as well as our mortality risk.

For some, making connections is easier said than done. There are those who consider themselves introverts they are people who are comfortable with being alone. This comfort, in many ways, can be an impediment to creating relationships that are critical for professional development and advancement. Also, when you have positive working relationships, you are able to focus your energy on opportunities rather than the impediments that can come with negative relationships.

What is the path forward for creating positive relationships? Here are five ways you can create opportunities to build authentic and meaningful relationships within your personal life and in the workplace.

- Create spaces that foster collaboration, connection, and community, and invite those who enter your spaces to do the same.
- Open your heart and mind to the thoughts and opinions of others, and encourage dialogue and conversations to share them.
- Create inclusive environments that allow you and those you connect with to engage in meaningful exchanges and share stories.
- Open yourself to listening to and appreciating the lived experiences of others, and understand how those lived experiences shape thoughts and actions.
- Listen actively, and with intent, to understand those you interact with, and encourage them to do the same with you.

These steps are relevant to building all relationships. They encourage you to open yourself to connecting with new people, and even reconnecting with those with whom you may have lost touch. They will bring positivity into your life and foster authentic relationships.

Here are some Coach Yourself Questions to help you build positive relationships

Which are the most important relationships that I have, and how have I built them?

What are important relationships that I should have but don't?

How can I work on building relationships with people I would benefit from being connected with?

What is the most meaningful and authentic relationship I have, and what makes it so?

What steps can I take to create more positive and meaningful relationships in my life and work?

Goals for building positive relationships

Now, let's set some goals around creating more positive relationships. Think about what you can realistically achieve in the time frame you've set for yourself. This could be over the next week, month, or several weeks. It is recommended that you identify at least three goals related to the five ways to create opportunities to build relationships described in the chapter.

Goal 1: _____

Goal 2: _____

Goal 3: _____

GOAL ACTION *plan*

GOAL

START: END:

. . . .

MOTIVATION

ACTION STEPS

START   COMPLETION

POSSIBLE OBSTACLES

OUTCOME

POSSIBLE SOLUTIONS

Be Well to Lead Well

GOAL ACTION *plan*

GOAL

START:　　　　END:

. . . .

MOTIVATION

ACTION STEPS

START　　COMPLETION

. . . .

. . . .

. . . .

. . . .

POSSIBLE OBSTACLES

OUTCOME

POSSIBLE SOLUTIONS

GOAL ACTION *plan*

GOAL

START: END:

. . . .

MOTIVATION

ACTION STEPS

START   COMPLETION

....

....

....

POSSIBLE OBSTACLES

OUTCOME

POSSIBLE SOLUTIONS

Be Well to Lead Well

Chapter 13

Operating in Optimism

"**Optimism is essential to achievement and it is also the foundation of courage and true progress.**"

— Nicholas M. Butler

Optimism, in its simplest definition, is the expectation of positive and desirable events in the future. It is looking toward the future through a lens of 'can and will rather than can't or won't.

Seeing and expecting outcomes to be favorable impact how we approach life and the decisions we make. As we lead in our homes, places of work, or at our businesses, a positive outlook concerning the future is what will drive us toward making the efforts needed to achieve the goals we set.

Being positive about achieving success and reaching our goals is what optimism is all about. Believing that good things will happen, no matter what, puts us in a psychological state of mind that will keep us striving to do our best all the time.

Studies have shown that not only does optimism lead to better career success, it also leaves an impact on better social functioning. Levels of optimism are also associated with our ability to get through adverse situations and can aid in creating a psychological shift in thinking and behavior that allows us to be successful.

Think of a highly memorable positive event that recently occurred in your life. It can be related to family, such as a reunion or family vacation, or it can be about a friendship, or even about an accomplishment at work. It can be any event that you would consider favorable.

Now, once you've recalled the details, be sure to remember them honestly. Recall the thoughts, feelings, and behaviors before, during, and after the event. Who was there? **Be as thorough as possible, and reflect on these questions.**

- What are some of the possible reasons and circumstances that led to the occurrence of this event?
- What are the reasons that you would give yourself credit for? What did you control?

- How was your control expressed and used to create or cause this positive event?

- What factors would you consider that were beyond your control?

- To what extent do you believe that external factors that contributed to the occurrence of this positive event?

- Of these external factors, which, if any, were within your control? If they were, how?

- If there were factors that you could have controlled but didn't, why didn't you? Optimism is all about looking toward the future, so, now, shift your perspective there. Thinking of the same positive event you've reflected on, can you reimagine it?

Now answer these questions.
- Do you believe that this positive event can happen again in the future?

- Thinking of the factors that you believe contributed to the positive event, both the ones inside and outside of your control, which ones do you believe will always exist, and which ones were happenstance?

- Considering the factors that you have just identified, do you believe they can be useful in other events or situations in your life?

- What would you do differently should you find yourself in the same situation in the future?

As optimists, we often explain positive events that occur in our lives as permanent and pervasive. We, in turn, interpret negative events as external, temporary, or specific to a situation.

Optimistic people take credit for the positive happenings in their lives, and the cause of desirable events as within their power and control. Having this positive view allows us to internalize the good aspects of our lives not only in the past, but the present and future as well.

Sometimes it can be challenging to remain optimistic when we are faced with adversity. However, when taking into consideration how those with high levels of optimism are able to see their contributions to positive outcomes, there is an almost automatic desire to strive for more positive outcomes. This leads to making decisions that lead to positive or desirable outcomes, not just some of the time, but all of the time. Whether they are decisions about your family, your home, your business, your career, or any other aspect of your life, expecting the good to happen often leads to it happening.

A word of caution: one thing to always remember is to not try to exert too much control. While we can control most of what impacts our lives, there are some aspects that aren't within our control. And, if we are not mindful of that, if we put too much pressure on ourselves, we can have undesirable outcomes.

Here are some Coach Yourself Questions to help you operate in optimism.

What has been the most recent positive event in my personal life? What was my contribution to its outcome?

What can I continue to do in my personal life to replicate positive outcomes?

What has been the most recent positive event in my work life? What was my contribution to its outcome?

What can I continue to do in my work life to replicate positive outcomes?

What are some things that I would like to change about my thoughts/ behaviors/actions to create continued positive outcomes in my life/ work?

Goals for operating in optimism

Now, let's set some goals around operating in optimism. Think about what you can realistically achieve in the time frame you've set for yourself. This could be over the next week, month, or several weeks. It is recommended that you identify at least one goal for creating more desirable outcomes in your home life and work life.

Goal 1: _____

Goal 2: _____

GOAL ACTION *plan*

GOAL

START: END:

. . . .

MOTIVATION

ACTION STEPS

START   COMPLETION

POSSIBLE OBSTACLES

OUTCOME

POSSIBLE SOLUTIONS

GOAL ACTION *plan*

GOAL

START: END:

. . . .

MOTIVATION

ACTION STEPS

START   COMPLETION

POSSIBLE OBSTACLES

OUTCOME

POSSIBLE SOLUTIONS

Be Well to Lead Well

Chapter 14

Being Hopeful

"The capacity for hope is the most significant fact of life. It provides human beings with a sense of destination and the energy to get started."

— Norman Cousins

Where there's a will, there's a way. It's an age old saying, but one that is often used casually without knowing its true meaning. In short, it means when an individual is determined to do something, they will find a way despite the obstacles that may try to prevent them from doing so. It is willpower and the path to achieve any goal you set for yourself. It is hope.

Hope is being determined, putting in the necessary time and energy, eliminating distractions, being up for whatever challenges, and seeing and setting the path to achieve your goals.

This sounds like a lot, but, when you really think about it, it's not as difficult as one may think. Hope is based on having a sense of successful goal directed energy and a plan to meet that goal. When we are able to reflect on circumstances, situations, and events that may not have gone in the direction we wanted, but we are able to identify a positive path forward, it can be said that we have a high level of hope. If you can't see a positive path forward, it doesn't mean that you lack hope or that such lack will impede your ability to perform at an optimal level, so don't get discouraged.

Like many other psychological attributes, hope is a state; it can change, and levels can be variable. To aid in the development and nurture of hope, there are eight approaches you can take.

Number one - Set Goals: Setting goals influences our levels of motivation, the choices we make, the level of energy we extend, how persistent we are, and, not only our willingness, but also our ability to find creative ways to achieve our goals.

Number two - Stretch Your Goals: Stretch goals are just challenging enough to stimulate excitement and exploration, but not too much of a challenge that they won't allow us to achieve them. They require a little extra effort but can help us discover potential we never knew we had.

Number three - Step Up Your Goals: Step up goals are long-term, challenging, and possibly overwhelming, but they take our goals to the next level. Stepping up goals actually forces us to take a step back and break down our goals into manageable milestones that will allow us to see success.

Number four - Involve Others: When we have the opportunity to share our goals with others, and to utilize the knowledge, support, and resources others can provide, garnering the willpower and seeing the way forward becomes less ominous because we know we are not alone.

Number five - Reward Yourself: Oftentimes, the hard work we do goes unnoticed both by ourselves and by those around us. Recognizing the achievement of an identified goal, either set by you or others, can be motivating.

Number six - Utilize Resources: Knowing what resources are available to us and utilizing those resources to achieve goals makes the acts associated with achieving those goals less daunting. This is because the idea of struggle is disheartening and can make us less hopeful in the positive outcomes we seek. When we know we have support, our outlook towards challenging tasks becomes more positive.

Number seven - Work in Your Strengths: Your goals should be aligned with your strengths. When you work in your strengths, there are a greater number of paths forward to choose from and, with options, success becomes inevitable.

Number eight - Upskill: Enhancing your general competencies and developing your talents into strengths allows you to become more adaptive to different situations and makes it easier to navigate difficult situations that would otherwise leave you feeling hopeless.

These eight approaches, while not exhaustive, can help you nurture and develop hope within yourself and lead you toward optimal performance whether it is at home or in the workplace.

Here are some Coach Yourself Questions to help you be more hopeful.

How do I proactively determine the way to accomplish my goals?

What is my process for figuring out and evaluating alternative paths to achieving my goals?

When I am challenged, or when my efforts to achieve my goals are marred with obstacles, have I already identified alternatives to circumvent the obstacles? What is my process for doing so?

Do I have strengths to draw from to manage around my areas of weakness and vulnerability? How do I use those strengths to ensure I am successful in achieving my goals?

Goals for being hopeful

Now, let's set some goals around being more hopeful. Think about what you can realistically achieve in the time frame you've set for yourself. This could be over the next week, month, or several weeks. It is recommended that you identify at least three goals related to the eight approaches to develop and nurture hope described in the chapter.

Goal 1: _____

Goal 2: _____

Goal 3: _____

GOAL ACTION *plan*

GOAL

START: END:

. . . .

MOTIVATION

ACTION STEPS

START   COMPLETION

POSSIBLE OBSTACLES

OUTCOME

POSSIBLE SOLUTIONS

GOAL ACTION *plan*

GOAL

. . . .

MOTIVATION

ACTION STEPS

START   COMPLETION

....

....

....

....

POSSIBLE OBSTACLES

OUTCOME

POSSIBLE SOLUTIONS

GOAL ACTION *plan*

GOAL

START: END:

. . . .

MOTIVATION

ACTION STEPS

START   COMPLETION

POSSIBLE OBSTACLES

OUTCOME

POSSIBLE SOLUTIONS

Be Well to Lead Well

Chapter 15

Staying Motivated

"Limitations live only in our minds. But if we use our imaginations, our possibilities become limitless."

— Jamie Paolinetti

Be Well to Lead Well

Work can become overwhelming sometimes. More often than not, we can be consumed by it, and in turn become demotivated.

This happens for many reasons including:

- not seeing how the work we do contributes to the bigger picture of our organization.
- not being recognized for the work we do, and, in turn, feeling devalued.
- not utilizing or underutilizing our strengths.
- working in ways that perpetuate burnout rather than promote well-being.

Mantras, affirmations, sayings, quotes, poems, and all of the written and spoken forms of art have always been tools proven to lift the spirit, inspire, and motivate people.

Here are five mantras to help you get past some of the things that can deter you from being engaged. These will keep you motivated at work and help you create an environment that allows you to be productive and work with purpose and intention.

Number one: Today I approach my work with enthusiasm and excitement knowing that my contributions are valuable and have a positive impact.

Number two: Today I bring positive energy into my work space and create an environment that is encouraging to my professional development and growth.

Number three: Today I focus on my successes and use them as a guide to continue to do work that is meaningful and rewarding.

Number four: Today I seek out new and exciting opportunities to increase my knowledge, skills, and abilities to grow professionally and reach the goals I have set for myself.

Number five: Today I work in my strengths, and use them to design a work experience that promotes productivity, well-being, and satisfaction.

These mantras can be repeated every day or as often as you need to be motivated to do work that is meaningful and impactful. They will remind you of the value and talent you possess and bring with you to work every day. They will also bring positivity and encouragement to keep the momentum you need to succeed.

Here are some Coach Yourself Questions to help stay motivated.

How does my work contribute to the bigger picture of my organization/company?

What value do I bring to my team and my workplace?

What are some new and exciting opportunities I can seek out to grow professionally?

How can I utilize my strengths to create a work experience that promotes productivity, well-being and satisfaction?

Goals for staying motivated

Now, let's set some goals around staying motivated. Think about what you can realistically achieve in the time frame you've set for yourself. This could be over the next week, month, or several weeks. It is recommended that you identify at least three goals related to the five mantras described in the chapter.

Goal 1: _____

Goal 2: _____

Goal 3: _____

GOAL ACTION *plan*

GOAL

START: END:

. . . .

MOTIVATION

ACTION STEPS

START   COMPLETION

POSSIBLE OBSTACLES

OUTCOME

POSSIBLE SOLUTIONS

GOAL ACTION *plan*

GOAL

START: END:

. . . .

MOTIVATION

ACTION STEPS

START   COMPLETION

....

....

....

....

POSSIBLE OBSTACLES

OUTCOME

POSSIBLE SOLUTIONS

GOAL ACTION *plan*

GOAL

START: END:

. . . .

MOTIVATION

ACTION STEPS

START   COMPLETION

POSSIBLE OBSTACLES

OUTCOME

POSSIBLE SOLUTIONS

Concluding Reflection

This book is called Be Well to Lead Well. In order for us to lead personal and work lives and careers that are happy, healthy, productive, and impactful, we need to be well as individuals and professionals. The goal of this book was to set you on the path to doing so. The aim was to provide you with time and space to reflect on core areas of development that support personal and professional growth. Life can be challenging. Work can be challenging. But if we have the tools we need to meet those challenges head-on, nothing can stop us from becoming the self-actualized humans we all strive to be. Actively working on ourselves and prioritizing well-being in every part of our lives is what creates true success.

Be Well to Lead Well

CHALLENGE

The work toward becoming the best version of yourself should never stop. You should constantly and consistently engage in activities that help you develop as a person and as a professional. To help encourage you to continue your growth, here is a 15-Day workplace well-being challenge focused on enhancing what you have already learned and to put into practice even more ways to be well at work.

Each day of the challenge focuses on one of the areas of the chapters in the book. Each day has three recommended activities and one journal prompt associated with it. Journaling has been proven to have many benefits including reducing stress and anxiety, improving awareness and perception, regulating emotions, and improving physical health. These are all things we need to show up, be productive, and make an impact in our lives and work.

For each day, complete at least one of the suggested activities and the journal prompt. For each activity you complete, take some time to reflect on the thoughts and feelings associated with it.

Use the space provided in the book, or your own journal, to keep track of what you've done and how it has made you feel. You may also find it beneficial to have an accountability partner; this is someone to keep you motivated, and to make sure you stay on track. Maybe they can even do the challenge with you.

At the end of the challenge, celebrate! Even the small wins matter.

Day 1: Developing Psychosocial Well-being

Activity 1: Practice mindfulness for 10 minutes.

Reflection: _____
_____
_____
_____
_____

Activity 2: Identify and challenge one negative thought.

Reflection: _____
_____
_____
_____
_____

Activity 3: Connect with a coworker, and share one thing you appreciate about them.

Reflection: _____
_____
_____
_____
_____

Journal Prompt

Reflect on a recent work-related challenge. How did you cope with it emotionally? What strategies helped you manage your feelings?

_____

_____

_____

_____

_____

_____

_____

_____

_____

_____

_____

_____

_____

_____

_____

_____

_____

_____

Day 2: Caring for Yourself

Activity 1: Take a 15-minute break outside.

Reflection: _____

_____

_____

_____

_____

Activity 2: Prepare and enjoy a healthy lunch.

Reflection: _____

_____

_____

_____

_____

Activity 3: Engage in a relaxing activity after work (e.g., reading, listening to music, taking a bath).

Reflection: _____

_____

_____

_____

_____

Journal Prompt

Describe one self-care habit you would like to prioritize this month.
How do you think it will positively impact your work performance?

_____

_____

_____

_____

_____

_____

_____

_____

_____

_____

_____

_____

_____

_____

_____

_____

_____

_____

Day 3: Creating Work–Life Synergy

Activity 1: Set boundaries by establishing a designated workspace.

Reflection: _____

_____

_____

_____

_____

Activity 2: Create a daily schedule that includes time for work, exercise, relaxation, and personal activities.

Reflection: _____

_____

_____

_____

_____

Activity 3: Have a technology-free evening and spend quality time with loved ones.

Reflection: _____

_____

_____

_____

_____

Journal Prompt

Reflect on how integrating work and personal life has affected your overall well-being. What adjustments can you make to achieve better synergy?

_____

_____

_____

_____

_____

_____

_____

_____

_____

_____

_____

_____

_____

_____

_____

_____

_____

Day 4: Getting Rid of
Self-Sabotaging Thoughts

Activity 1: Practice positive affirmations for 5 minutes.

Reflection: _____

_____

_____

_____

_____

Activity 2: Challenge a limiting belief by reframing it in a more empowering way.

Reflection: _____

_____

_____

_____

_____

Activity 3: Visualize yourself succeeding in a challenging situation.

Reflection: _____

_____

_____

_____

_____

Journal Prompt

Identify one self-sabotaging thought pattern you tend to experience at work. How can you actively work to change this mindset?

_____

_____

_____

_____

_____

_____

_____

_____

_____

_____

_____

_____

_____

_____

_____

_____

_____

Day 5: Creating a Personal Mission

Activity 1: Reflect on your values, and write down what matters most to you in your career.

Reflection: _____

_____

_____

_____

_____

Activity 2: Define your long-term career goals and aspirations.

Reflection: _____

_____

_____

_____

_____

Activity 3: Draft a personal mission statement that aligns with your values and goals.

Reflection: _____

_____

_____

_____

_____

Journal Prompt

Share your personal mission statement, and explain how it guides your actions and decisions in the workplace.

Day 6: Strengthening Your Self-Efficacy

Activity 1: Set a small, achievable goal for the day, and accomplish it.

Reflection: _____

_____

_____

_____

_____

Activity 2: Recall a past success and reflect on the skills and strengths you utilized.

Reflection: _____

_____

_____

_____

_____

Activity 3: Seek feedback from a colleague or supervisor and acknowledge areas where you excel.

Reflection: _____

_____

_____

_____

_____

Be Well to Lead Well

Journal Prompt

Describe a recent accomplishment at work that boosted your
confidence. How can you leverage this experience to
tackle future challenges?

_____

_____

_____

_____

_____

_____

_____

_____

_____

_____

_____

_____

_____

_____

_____

Day 7: Recognizing Your Strengths

Activity 1: Complete a strengths assessment tool (e.g., StrengthsFinder, VIA Character Survey).

Reflection: _____

_____

_____

_____

_____

Activity 2: List three strengths you possess and examples of how you've utilized them in your role.

Reflection: _____

_____

_____

_____

_____

Activity 3: Express gratitude for a colleague's strengths and how they contribute to the team.

Reflection: _____

_____

_____

_____

_____

Journal Prompt

Reflect on how recognizing and leveraging your strengths can enhance your job satisfaction and performance.

Day 8: Building Resilience

Activity 1: Practice deep breathing, or a relaxation technique, during a stressful moment.

Reflection: _____

_____

_____

_____

_____

Activity 2: Reflect on a past challenge you've overcome and how it has made you stronger.

Reflection: _____

_____

_____

_____

_____

Activity 3: Reach out to a mentor or supportive colleague for advice or encouragement.

Reflection: _____

_____

_____

_____

_____

Journal Prompt

How did practicing resilience techniques help you navigate
challenges more effectively today?

_____

_____

_____

_____

_____

_____

_____

_____

_____

_____

_____

_____

_____

_____

_____

_____

_____

Day 9: Overcoming Overwhelm

Activity 1: Prioritize your tasks identifying what is urgent and what is important.

Reflection: _____

_____

_____

_____

_____

Activity 2: Break down overwhelming tasks into smaller, actionable steps.

Reflection: _____

_____

_____

_____

_____

Activity 3: Delegate tasks where possible and ask for help if needed.

Reflection: _____

_____

_____

_____

_____

Journal Prompt

How did utilizing time management strategies help you regain a sense of control and reduce overwhelm today?

_____

_____

_____

_____

_____

_____

_____

_____

_____

_____

_____

_____

_____

_____

_____

_____

_____

_____

Day 10: Achieving Flow

Activity 1: Identify a task that you enjoy and that challenges you just enough.

Reflection: _____

_____

_____

_____

_____

Activity 2: Eliminate distractions and fully immerse yourself in a task for 30 minutes.

Reflection: _____

_____

_____

_____

_____

Activity 3: Reflect on how it feels to be in a state of flow, and how you can incorporate more of it into your work.

Reflection: _____

_____

_____

_____

_____

Journal Prompt

How did achieving a state of flow positively impact your productivity and enjoyment of your work today?

_____

_____

_____

_____

_____

_____

_____

_____

_____

_____

_____

_____

_____

_____

_____

_____

Day 11: Managing Yourself Through Change

Activity 1: Practice self-compassion by acknowledging your feelings about the change.

Reflection: _____

_____

_____

_____

_____

Activity 2: Identify the opportunities that come with the change and focus on them.

Reflection: _____

_____

_____

_____

_____

Activity 3: Seek support from colleagues or a mentor to navigate the transition.

Reflection: _____

_____

_____

_____

_____

Journal Prompt

How did practicing self-compassion and focusing on opportunities, help you adapt to change more effectively today?

_____

_____

_____

_____

_____

_____

_____

_____

_____

_____

_____

_____

_____

_____

_____

Day 12: Building Positive Relationships

Activity 1: Initiate a conversation with a coworker you don't know well.

Reflection: _____

_____

_____

_____

_____

Activity 2: Practice active listening during meetings or conversations.

Reflection: _____

_____

_____

_____

_____

Activity 3: Offer genuine compliments or expressions of appreciation to colleagues.

Reflection: _____

_____

_____

_____

_____

Journal Prompt

How did nurturing positive relationships contribute to a supportive
and collaborative work environment today?

_____

_____

_____

_____

_____

_____

_____

_____

_____

_____

_____

_____

_____

_____

_____

Day 13: Operating in Optimism

Activity 1: Start your day by setting a positive intention.

Reflection: _____

_____

_____

_____

_____

Activity 2: Look for the silver lining in challenges or setbacks.

Reflection: _____

_____

_____

_____

_____

Activity 3: Visualize a successful outcome for a project or task.

Reflection: _____

_____

_____

_____

_____

Journal Prompt

How did maintaining an optimistic outlook contribute to your
resilience and problem-solving abilities today?

_____

_____

_____

_____

_____

_____

_____

_____

_____

_____

_____

_____

_____

_____

_____

_____

_____

_____

_____

Day 14: Being Hopeful

Activity 1: Reflect on your long-term goals and aspirations.

Reflection: _____

_____

_____

_____

_____

Activity 2: Identify one small step you can take today to move closer to your goals.

Reflection: _____

_____

_____

_____

_____

Activity 3: Visualize yourself achieving your goals, and focus on the feelings of hope and excitement.

Reflection: _____

_____

_____

_____

_____

Journal Prompt

How did cultivating a sense of hopefulness motivate you to
take action towards your goals today?

_____

_____

_____

_____

_____

_____

_____

_____

_____

_____

_____

_____

_____

_____

_____

_____

Day 15: Staying Motivated

Activity 1: Create a vision board or visual representation of your goals and aspirations.

Reflection: _____

_____

_____

_____

_____

Activity 2: Set achievable goals for the day and reward yourself for completing them.

Reflection: _____

_____

_____

_____

_____

Activity 3: Reflect on your accomplishments and progress towards your long-term goals.

Reflection: _____

_____

_____

_____

_____

Journal Prompt

How did staying motivated and focused on your goals contribute to
your overall well-being and sense of fulfillment in your work?

_____

_____

_____

_____

_____

_____

_____

_____

_____

_____

_____

_____

_____

_____

_____

_____

References and Resources

Introduction

10 Ways to promote Occupational wellness https://www.togetherplatform.com/blog/promote-occupational-wellness

Batista, Ed. (2013). Self-coaching: an Overview https://www.edbatista.com/2013/07/self-coaching-an-overview.html

Neuhaus Ph.D., Maike (2021) Self-coaching model. 56 questions & Tools https://positivepsychology.com/self-coaching-model/

Peterson, Thad. "Bringing your whole self to work": What the hell does that mean

https://www.predictiveindex.com/blog/bringing-your-whole-self-to-work-what-the-hell-does-that-mean/

Robins, Mike. (2015). Bring your Whole Self to work : https://mike-robbins.com/tedxberkeley /

Tupper, Helen and Ellis, Sarah. (2022). How to become your own career coach https://hbr.org/2022/01/how-to-become-your-own-career-coach

Chapter 1 - Developing Psychosocial Wellbeing

Celestine, Ph.D, Nicole. (2021) The Ryff Scales of Psychological Wellbeing https://positivepsychology.com/ryff-scale-psychological-wellbeing/

Ryff CD. Psychological well-being revisited: advances in the science and practice of eudaimonia. Psychother Psychosom. 2014;83(1):10-28. doi: 10.1159/000353263. Epub 2013 Nov 19. PMID: 24281296; PMCID: PMC4241300. https://www.ncbi.nlm.nih.gov/pmc/articles/PMC4241300/

Wellness vs Wellbeing https://www.gallup.com/workplace/340202/wellness-wellbeing-difference.aspx

Chapter 2 - Caring for Yourself

American Psychological Association: Self-Care https://www.apa.org/research-practice/self-care

Anna Katharina Schaffner, Ph.D. (2020) How to Practice Self-Care: 10+ Worksheets and 12 Ideas https://positivepsychology.com/self-care-worksheets/

Caring for Your Mental Health https://www.nimh.nih.gov/health/topics/caring-for-your-mental-health

Chapter 3 - Creating Work-Life Synergy

Balance? What about work-life synergy? (2020) https://medium.com/@coachpadraig/balance-what-about-work-life-synergy-6e03aff26e27

Strive for Work-life Effectiveness. Not Balance https://www.idealist.org/en/careers/strive-for-work-life-effectiveness-rather-than-balance

Small, Ph.D., Waajida L. (2022). Work-Life | It's Not a Balance, It's Synergy https://www.idealist.org/en/careers/work-life-synergy

Chapter 4 - Getting Rid of Self-Sabotaging Thoughts

Bailey, James R. and Mezias, John M. (2022). 5 Self-Sabotaging Traps to Avoid at Work https://hbr.org/2022/06/5-self-sabotaging-traps-to-avoid-at-work

Christina R. Wilson, Ph.D. (2021). What Is Self-Sabotage? How to Help Stop the Vicious Cycle. https://positivepsychology.com/self-sabotage/

Field, Barbara. (2023). Self-Sabotaging: Why Does It Happen https://www.verywellmind.com/why-people-self-sabotage-and-how-to-stop-it-5207635

Self-Sabotage: Overcoming Self-Defeating Behavior https://www.mindtools.com/ano939l/self-sabotage

Chapter 5 - Creating a Personal Mission

Mind Tools Content Team. Personal Mission Statements https://www.mindtools.com/axcp8p5/personal-mission-statements

Chapter - 6 Strengthening Your Self-Efficacy

Luthans, F., Youssef, C. M., & Avolio, B. J. (2007). Psychological capital: Developing the human competitive edge. Oxford University Press.

Sorenson, Susan How Employees' Strengths Make Your Company Stronge   https://www.gallup.com/workplace/231605/employees-strengths-company-stronger.aspx

Chapter 7 - Recognizing Your Strengths

Buckingham, Marcus. (2019). 3 proven ways to win at work, says world-renowned talent expert. https://www.cnbc.com/2019/01/14/marcus-buckingham-3-scientifically-proven-ways-to-win-at-work.html

Clifton, Jim. (2022). Build Your Career Around Your Strengths, Not Your Weaknesses. https://www.gallup.com/workplace/402500/build-career-around-strengths-not-weaknesses.aspx

Use the CliftonStrengths Assessment to Discover & Develop Your Greatest Talents https://www.gallup.com/cliftonstrengths/en/253676/how-cliftonstrengths-works.aspx

Chapter 8 - Building Resilience

American Psychological Association.(2020). Building your resilience.

https://www.apa.org/topics/resilience/building-your-resilience

Doll, Psy.D., L.P. ,Karen. (2019). 23 Resilience Building Activities & Exercises for Adults.https://positivepsychology.com/resilience-activities-exercises/

Duszynski-Goodman, Lizzie . (2023). What Is Resilience? How To Build Resiliency, Benefits And More. https://www.forbes.com/health/mind/resilience/

Rainey, Cheri. (2023). Building Resilience In The Workplace: Strategies For Success. https://www.forbes.com/sites/forbescoachescouncil/2023/07/11/building-resilience-in-the-workplace-strategies-for-success/?sh=2ce822637bca

Chapter 9 - Overcoming Overwhelm

Rubenstein Ph.D, Carolyn.Tips to Help Overcome Overwhelmhttps://www.psychologytoday.com/us/blog/now-is-everything/202111/tips-help-overcome-overwhelm

Zucke, Rebecca (2019) How to Deal with Constantly Feeling Overwhelmed https://hbr.org/2019/10/how-to-deal-with-constantly-feeling-overwhelmed

Chapter 10 - Achieving Flow

Antonini Philippe R, Singer SM, Jaeger JEE, Biasutti M, Sinnett S. Achieving Flow: An Exploratory Investigation of Elite College Athletes and Musicians. Front Psychol. 2022 Mar 30;13:831508. doi: 10.3389/fpsyg.2022.831508. PMID: 35432058; PMCID: PMC9009586.

Cherry, MSEd Kendra. (2023). How to Achieve a State of Flow. https://www.verywellmind.com/what-is-flow-2794768

Cooks-Campbell, Allaya. (2022). Achieving a flow state: 7 ways to get in the zone. https://www.betterup.com/blog/flow-state

Chapter 11 - Managing Yourself Through Change

Clubb, Kathryn and Fan, Jeni. (2021). How to Become More Comfortable with Changehttps://hbr.org/2021/11/how-to-become-more-comfortable-with-change

Chapter 12 - Building Positive Relationships

Cherry, MSEd Kendra. (2023). How to Achieve a State of Flow. https://www.verywellmind.com/what-is-flow-2794768

Houston, B.Sc, Elaine (2019). The Importance of Positive Relationships in the Workplace https://positivepsychology.com/positive-relationships-workplace/

Seppälä, Emma and McNichols, Nicole K. (2022) The Power of Healthy Relationships at Work. https://hbr.org/2022/06/the-power-of-healthy-relationships-at-work

Chapter 13 - Operating in Optimism

Davis, Ph.D., Tchiki . (2021). 4 Tips to Be More Optimistic. https://www.psychologytoday.com/us/blog/click-here-happiness/202105/4-tips-be-more-optimistic

Morin, LCSW, Amy. (2022). Being Optimistic When the World Around You Isn't. https://www.verywellmind.com/how-to-be-optimistic-4164832

Scott, PhD , Elizabeth. (2020). 5 Steps to Being More of an Optimist https://www.verywellmind.com/become-more-of-an-optimist-3144818

Chapter 14 - Being Hopeful

Haupt, Angela. (2023). How to Cultivate Hope When You Don't Have Any. https://time.com/6327444/how-to-be-more-hopeful/

Jensen, Dane. (2022). Sustaining Hope in Uncertain Times. https://hbr.org/2022/03/sustaining-hope-in-uncertain-times?utm_medium=paidsearch&utm_source=google&utm_campaign=domcontent&utm_term=Non-Brand&tpcc=paidsearch.google.dsacontent&gad_source=1&gclid=CjwKCAiAt5euBhB9EiwAdkXWOyt9ve-OZYGduNYKMp5DpMWoMmWizOOYdbZfJUgl2WbiapEdBYMZTRoCwTgQAvD_BwE

Chapter 15 - Staying Motivated

Cascio CN, O'Donnell MB, Tinney FJ, Lieberman MD, Taylor SE, Strecher VJ, Falk EB. Self-affirmation activates brain systems associated with self-related processing and reward and is reinforced by future orientation. Soc Cogn Affect Neurosci. 2016 Apr;11(4):621-9. doi: 10.1093/scan/nsv136. Epub 2015 Nov 5. PMID: 26541373; PMCID:

Be Well to Lead Well

PMC4814782.

Moore, Catherine (2019). Positive Daily Affirmations: Is There Science Behind It?. https://positivepsychology.com/daily-affirmations/

About the Author

Dr. Waajida Small is an award-winning HR executive and Founder, CEO of Capital Conscious U LLC, a leadership development firm focused on helping women find and align their purpose with their life and work, lead authentically, and make an impact. She is the author of "Our Leadership Journey: Shared Stories, Lessons, and Advice for Women of Color" and contributing author to the Amazon best-selling book" Women Connected in Wisdom Volume II: Stories and Resources Rooted in the 8 Dimensions of Wellness". Dr. Small is a certified professional coach with specialties in life, leadership, career, and executive coaching. She holds a doctorate degree in Human Capital Management with a research emphasis on women and leadership.

For almost two decades as a human resources leader and executive, Dr. Small has helped international organizations design and implement strategies to attract, develop, and retain top talent.

Her purpose is to help cultivate other purpose driven leaders who create spaces for women to be successful and provide value to the world and those they serve. She does this by sharing her knowledge, wisdom, and experience, through coaching, and by teaching strategies and best practices to position women for success.

Be Well to Lead Well

www.ingramcontent.com/pod-product-compliance
Lightning Source LLC
Chambersburg PA
CBHW071157130626
46553CB00004B/1699